LANGUAGE FOR YOUR PURPOSE

Spoken Words of Identity, Healing, and Beauty

By Patricia A. Haynes

LANGUAGE FOR YOUR PURPOSE

Spoken Words of Identity, Healing, and Beauty

Copyright © 2025 by **Patricia A. Haynes**
All rights reserved.

No part of this book may be reproduced or transmitted in any form or by any means, electronic or mechanical, including photocopying, recording, or by any information storage and retrieval system, without written permission from the publisher, except in the case of brief quotations embodied in reviews.

ISBN: 979-8-9941528-0-5
Publisher: Haynes Legacy Press
Printed in the United States of America.
Scripture quotations are taken from the Holy Bible, NIV, NLT, NKJV as indicated.

Dedication

To God—my Keeper, my Father, my Source...

To my husband, Carlton—my answered prayer, my partner in peace...

To my children and grandchildren—my reasons, my joy, my legacy...

To my sweet Mommie Girlie—whose strength shaped mine...

To my dearest sisters in love (law), Jay, CiCi, and spiritual sister Ruthie, thank you for walking with me.

And to every woman who has ever fought her way back to purpose.

May you always remember:

You are seen. You are loved. You are becoming

Prologue

There are moments in life when God whispers long before we recognize His voice, guiding us gently through storms we didn't choose and victories we didn't see coming. My story didn't begin with clarity or confidence — it began with a little girl learning to listen.

I grew up surrounded by poverty, silence, secrets, and spiritual shadows, yet even then, God was speaking — not loudly, but consistently. Through every season, He was giving me language for my purpose before I had the words to describe it.

This book is not just a memoir.

It is a testimony.

A revelation.

A journey through identity, healing, and beauty.

It is the unfolding of a woman shaped by God's hands, refined by struggle, and restored by grace.

To every woman who has ever asked,

"Who am I beyond what life has done to me?"

this book is my answer — and yours.

Come closer.

Lean in.

Listen.

There is beauty in your becoming.

A Note to My Younger Self

My sweet girl…

you worried about things that were never meant to define you.

You carried burdens too heavy, secrets too dark, questions too deep.

But hear me now:

You survived every moment that tried to silence you.

You overcame every lie that tried to shrink you.

You grew into a woman you would be proud of — strong, whole, healed, and beautiful.

The future is bright.

The darkness will fade.

And every tear you cried watered the garden of the woman you became.

Hold on.

God is shaping you.

Introduction

Language is powerful.

It shapes how we see the world, how we interpret pain, how we rise from what tried to break us, and how we walk into purpose. But what happens when you grow up without the right language — for identity, for love, for trauma, for God, or even for yourself?

You learn it.

Slowly.

Tenderly.

Sometimes painfully.

Always purposefully.

This book is the language I learned along the way —

the language God whispered through storms, through silence, through heartbreak, through resilience, through revelation.

Each chapter is a piece of my becoming.

Each testimony is a stone laid on the path God built for me.

Each scripture is a breath of truth anchoring my journey.

I share my life not to expose, but to illuminate.

Not to relive, but to release.

Not to impress, but to inspire.

If my story helps you name your own…

If my healing helps ignite yours…

If my voice awakens yours…

then this book has fulfilled its purpose.

Come with me.

Let's walk through identity, healing, and beauty — together.

Contents

Dedication i
Prologue ii
A Note to My Younger Self iii
Introduction iv
Contents v
Chapter 1 — Lean In, Come Closer 1
Chapter 2 — Shhh! Don't Tell 4
Chapter 3 — I Didn't Get What I Needed 8
Chapter 4 — My Mommie Girl 11
Chapter 5 — Oops! I Did It Again 16
Chapter 6 — Missing Ingredients 20
Chapter 7 — Finding My Voice 24
Chapter 8 — Standing in the Gap 28
Chapter 9 — More Than a Woman 33
Chapter 10 — Problem to Purpose 37
Chapter 11 — Shaping Faith 41
Chapter 12 — Turning Struggle Into Strength 46
Chapter 13 — Partnership & Peace 51
Chapter 14 — Peeling the Promises 55
Chapter 15 — Seeing the Blessings of God 60
Chapter 16 — Built for B-E-A-U-T-Y 64

Scripture Index 69
About the Author 71

CHAPTER 1
Lean In — Come Closer

Not because my story is perfect, but because it is honest. Come closer because every chapter of my life carries a whisper of God's hand, even the parts I tried to ignore, outrun, or forget. If you lean in long enough, you may hear an echo of your own story resting inside mine.

I grew up in a place where silence had its own sound, a quiet so thick it carried the weight of truth no one dared to name. Mississippi was beautiful in its own way, but beauty can sit right beside brokenness without ever apologizing. Our little town was stitched together with dirt roads, worn porches, and people who learned to make life out of whatever they had left. Poverty wasn't just around us; it was inside the structure of our days in the cold winter nights with no heat, in the mornings when the water wouldn't run, in the meals stretched thinner than our hope.

But even then... I was paying attention.

I watched the way adults whispered when things went wrong, how truth was encouraged until it brushed up against family secrets. If the law came knocking, or if someone you loved crossed lines that couldn't be explained away, silence became a survival strategy. "Don't tell nobody," they'd say. "That stays in this house." And so, I learned to hold truths bigger than a child should carry.

But God was already teaching me to lean in.

I leaned in when my mother left for work, trusting me to care for my siblings.

I leaned in when darkness crept into my room and spirits hovered in corners, only to retreat when the presence of God wrapped around me like a blanket.

I leaned in when I had no father to lean on, building strength in the space where guidance should have been.

There was something inside me — a knowing, a weight, a whisper telling me that my life had language long before I learned to speak it.

While other kids ran free during summer evenings, I sat quietly watching, listening, and learning. I studied the patterns of people. I noticed emotions before I had the words to name them. I paid attention to the stillness of moments most children wouldn't recognize. While they played, I practiced sewing with tiny fingers, humming songs under my breath, dancing when joy found its way to me. I wasn't isolated; I was being shaped.

Purpose often starts as a whisper.

And when you grow up in survival mode, whispers are easy to miss — but impossible to forget.

There were days I wondered why I felt "different," why I carried more responsibility, more awareness, more weight than those around me. I didn't yet understand that sensitivity was a spiritual gift, that discernment can develop in children who experience too much too early, and that leadership is often birthed in silence.

I learned to read rooms because sometimes reading people meant staying safe.

I learned to anticipate needs because someone had to.

I learned to be brave because bravery was the only option.

But through it all, I learned to lean in.

Lean into God's nudges.
Lean into the moments that didn't make sense.
Lean into the questions without answers.
Lean into the responsibility that rested on my shoulders like an early mantle.

Every chapter of my life begins with that simple invitation: **lean in.**

Because leaning in is what helped me see that God's hand never once left my life, not in the cold nights, not in the silent mornings, not in the secret moments when spiritual darkness tried to intimidate my purpose.

Come closer, reader.

I want to show you how a little girl from Mississippi learned to listen not to the noise around her,
but to the quiet calling within.

"The Lord is near to all who call on Him." — Psalm 145:18 (NIV)

Even when you didn't have the language for what you were feeling…
Even when you leaned in because life demanded it…
Even when you sat in silence, watching, listening, discerning…

God was near.

He was the presence in the cold nights,

the whisper in the quiet moments,

the shield against spiritual darkness,

the steady hand forming your purpose long before you recognized it.

CHAPTER 2
Shhh! Don't Tell

Silence has a sound.

Not the peaceful kind that settles over a quiet morning, but the kind that sits heavy on a child's chest pressing, shaping, warning. The kind of silence that teaches you what you can say... and what you must never say.

Growing up, I learned that truth had limits.

You could speak it freely until it threatened to unravel someone's comfort, reputation, or relationship. Then that truth became a secret, and secrets became currency.

"Don't tell nobody."

"Keep this between us."

"I'll buy you something if you stay quiet."

Candy.

Coins.

Little toys.

All handed to me like peace offerings for my silence.

I didn't know it then, but adults were asking me to protect their choices while I was still trying to understand my own world. I watched family members I trusted, people I held in high regard slip in and out of loyalty to the ones they professed to love. Affairs, broken promises, private meetings, hushed conversations... and the burden of those moments stacked inside my childhood like bricks.

And still, I kept quiet.

Not because I wanted to, but because I didn't know what else to do.

Then came the deeper secret—the one I didn't ask for, the one that carried weight beyond my understanding. The day I learned that my grandfather might not be my real grandfather, something inside me cracked. How do you question the man who made you feel like you were his favorite? How do you reconcile a truth that untangles your identity?

I wanted to ask him.
I wanted to understand.
But fear sat in my throat like a stone.

So, I watched.
I listened.
I noticed things in my grandparents' home, the subtle differences in how my mother was treated compared to her siblings. The way the air tightened when certain topics came up. The distance between my grandmother's heart and my mother's value. I didn't understand the history, but I saw the pain.

And somehow… I felt responsible for it.

Their home was the hub where we ate, where we played, where we gathered. But for me, it became a place of observation. I kept visiting, not because I always felt celebrated, but because I didn't want my mother to feel alone. I didn't want her to stand in the shadow of favoritism without someone standing beside her.

I thought I was protecting her even though I had never been protected from the truth.

When the confusion became too loud, I found my own ways to escape.
Music.
Cleaning.

Dancing.

Television.

Anything to redirect the thoughts swirling in my young mind. Anything to silence the questions I wasn't allowed to ask. Anything to keep the peace in a world where secrets could shift the entire atmosphere.

Looking back, I realize I wasn't just keeping secrets… I was carrying them.

Carrying my mother's hurt.

Carrying the weight of false loyalty.

Carrying the fear of losing the grandfather I cherished.

Carrying the confusion of being a child trapped in adult realities.

And if I could go back, if I could hold that younger version of myself, I would whisper to her:

"The future looks bright, baby.

The darkness you're in now will not last.

You will not stay in this silence forever."

Because even though I didn't know it then, God was already preparing me.

He was giving me spiritual hearing before I had natural understanding.

He was teaching me emotional discernment before I had language for it.

He was forming resilience in the very places where confusion tried to break me.

"Shhh! Don't Tell" wasn't just a rule in my childhood—it became the backdrop where God shaped the voice I would one day reclaim.

And now…

I speak.

I heal.

I write.

I tell.

Not to expose my family,
but to honor the girl who held their secrets
until she learned to hold her own purpose.

Scripture Reflection:

**"He reveals deep and secret things;
He knows what is in the darkness,
and the light dwells with Him."**

— Daniel 2:22 (NKJV)

CHAPTER 3
I Didn't Get What I Needed

There are some needs a child can't name, but their heart feels the absence long before their mind understands it. One of those needs is a father, not the idea of one, not the picture of one, not the letter-writing version of one… but the presence of one.

Growing up, I tried to fill that space with reasons.

Maybe he was busy.

Maybe he didn't know how to be a father.

Maybe I wasn't enough.

Maybe if I behaved well enough, helped enough, smiled enough, he would choose me.

I didn't know then that children often blame themselves for the decisions adults make long before they are born.

My siblings had their father, a man who wrapped me in love without hesitation. He never separated us, never divided his affection or his finances. When he bought items for them, he bought for me. When he hugged them, he hugged me. When he called them his children, he called me his daughter. It was the first time I felt what covering looked like, kindness without condition, love without boundaries.

And yet… the void remained.

Not because he didn't do enough.

Not because his love wasn't real.

But because the soul remembers its origins.

And my soul remembered a man I barely knew.

My siblings would tease me, maybe out of immaturity, maybe out of innocence, maybe out of not understanding my wound.

"You ain't got no daddy."

Words that pierced deeper than they realized.

I would laugh it off sometimes, pretend it didn't matter, pretend it didn't sting. But deep inside, something tightened. Something ached. Something whispered, "Why wasn't I enough for him to choose?"

I was a good girl.

Quiet.

Respectful.

Helpful.

Kind.

I didn't know what I had done wrong to be left.

I didn't understand why he sent pictures but never showed up.

I didn't understand why I could recognize his face yet not recognize his presence.

I didn't understand why the man in the photos, the man in uniform, the man smiling from a distance, wasn't walking through the door, choosing me, claiming me.

It wasn't until years later that I realized something important:

His absence shaped me, but it did not define me.

Still, as a child, absence feels like rejection.

And rejection feels like something you caused.

There were nights I imagined him showing up unexpectedly.

Days I imagined him calling my name.

Moments, I imagined him seeing me — truly seeing me — and deciding to stay.

But imagination can't heal what honesty uncovers:

I didn't get what I needed.

Not the affirmation.

Not the presence.

Not the father-daughter bond that steadies a girl's sense of worth.

And yet, in the midst of that void, God sent a man, my siblings' father who filled the gap in ways he never had to. He didn't owe me anything, but he gave me something invaluable: a glimpse of what fatherly love could look like.

I didn't get what I needed from the man who helped bring me into this world…

but God made sure I wasn't left empty.

He placed people in my life who taught me that love doesn't have to come from blood to be real.

He placed strength in my heart that grew in the cracks of disappointment. He placed purpose in the space where rejection tried to take root.

I didn't get what I needed from my biological father,

but I got what I needed to become who I am.

And that is the holiness of God's design: He fills every void with purpose.

Scripture Reflection:

"**Though my father and mother forsake me, the Lord will take me in.**" **— Psalm 27:10 (ESV)**

CHAPTER 4
My Mommie Girlie

"The woman whose strength held me long before I understood my own."

I didn't realize how much of my mother's strength lived inside me until the day I woke up after giving birth to my first child.

The room was hazy.

My vision blurred.

My mind searched for something familiar in a world suddenly out of focus.

And there she was...

My Mommie Girl.

Standing beside me, gently rubbing my forehead with her soft, steady hand, the same hand that corrected me, guided me, fed me, prayed for me, and carried burdens she never voiced.

I blinked through the fog, trying to understand where I was, what had happened, and why there were blurry figures standing against the walls like quiet shadows.

Then a single thought rose, sharp and urgent:

Where is my baby?

In the movies, mothers are handed their newborns, placed on their chest, wrapped in warmth, welcomed into the world.

But my chest was empty.

My arms were empty.

And panic returned as I whispered again, "Where's my baby?"

My mother hesitated, not out of fear, but out of protection. She was trying to shield me from the shock and the pain I wasn't strong enough yet to bear.

She soothed my head and finally said:

"He had some complications, baby… They had to fly him to Le Bonheur Children's Hospital. But listen to me, "*he is beautiful.*" Bright eyes. Full of joy. And "*he's going to be alright*". You just need to get stronger so you can go see him."

I learned later that I had been unconscious for three days. An asthma attack had taken me under, and I missed the beginning of my son's battle for life…

a battle he fought with Constriction Ring Syndrome, where amniotic bands wrapped around his developing limbs, leaving permanent differences.

But when I opened my eyes…

my mother was there.

Present.

Steady.

Silent in her own suffering, but unshakable in mine.

And that was my mother's love…

never loud when life required quiet,

never weak when life demanded strength,

never absent when her children were in need.

The Woman Behind the Strength

People have often described my mother as a "fusser,"

a "pop-off queen,"

someone who is too blunt, too loud, too much.

But they never saw the nights she cried behind closed doors.
They never saw the burdens she carried quietly so her children didn't have to.
They never saw the storms she survived just to keep loving, keep giving, keep showing up.

My mother is not a perfect woman.

She is a chosen woman.

Anointed.

Appointed.

Equipped with a spirit that refuses to bow to life's cruelty.

Family members sometimes avoided her, excluded her, whispered about her tone or her reactions.
But what they failed to understand is this:

When a woman has carried the weight of generations,
her strength can be mistaken for anger,
her voice mistaken for volume,
her boundaries mistaken for attitude.

My Mommie Girl learned early that if you "mash the button," you might receive a truth you weren't prepared to hear.

But behind that truth was a heart that loved fiercely,
a heart that gave too much,
served too much,
and cared too deeply for too many years to count.

She has spent more than 30 years caring for family members, including my three cousins with Fetal Alcohol Spectrum Disorders—loving them, protecting them, guiding them into adulthood with a patience most of us could never muster.

She did all of this while battling her own health issues, heartbreaks, disappointments, and silent prayers.

And still—

she stood.

She kept standing.

She still stands.

What I See Now

Growing up, I didn't always understand her.

I didn't always interpret her reactions correctly.

I didn't always recognize the weight she carried.

But now…

as a woman,

a mother,

a wife,

a grandmother…

I see her.

I see her sacrifices.

I see her tears.

I see her resilience.

I see her beauty.

I see her faith.

I see her humanness.

And I see the woman whose strength flows through my veins.

Mommie Girlie,

I see you through the trials, through the storms, through the spiritual battles others never knew you fought!

Your love is not always quiet.

Your strength is not always soft.

Your presence is not always understood.

But your resilience? Your heart? Your devotion?

They shine.

They shaped me.

They live in me.

And I am your daughter.

Scripture Reflection:

"Her children arise and call her blessed."

— Proverbs 31:28 (NIV)

CHAPTER 5
Oops! I Did It Again — Water-Falling Seasons

There are seasons in life when mistakes don't come one at a time, they come like water falling from a broken faucet,
drop after drop,
moment after moment,
until you find yourself drenched in choices you never meant to make.

This was one of those seasons.

Just when I thought I was finally pulling my life together, growing as a young mother, learning responsibility, doing the best I knew how…
I fell into another trap dressed up like affection.

I met him while working at a factory in Batesville, Mississippi, sewing elastic on men's and boys' briefs.
It wasn't glamorous work, but it was honest work. I was making my way, taking care of my child, finding my footing in the world.

Then he walked in.
Flirty.
Athletic.
Charming in all the ways I didn't realize were dangerous.
He made me feel seen at a time when I still didn't know how to see myself.

I didn't know it then, but I was still searching for something to fill the voids left by a father who wasn't there and a boy who never loved me back.
And when you're thirsty for affection, even poison can taste like water.

I fell for the okeydokey, the same trap millions of women fall into: a broken man with a beautiful smile.

It didn't take long before the truth came out:

He was married.

But instead of running, I stayed.

Instead of choosing wisdom, I chose fantasy.

Instead of stepping away, I stepped further in, believing every lie that came wrapped in apology and flattery.

He told me he filed for divorce.

He told me he wanted a life with me.

He told me I was different—special—chosen.

And I believed him.

If I had known then what I know now,

I would have run.

I would have waited.

I would have protected my heart instead of abandoning it.

But at that time, I thought love was something you fought for— even if it wasn't yours to fight for.

Too soon, we married.

Too soon, I stepped into a blended family.

Too soon, I uprooted my life, moved to Memphis, Tennessee, and tried to build a future on a cracked foundation.

The charming athlete became a man who lied,

laughed behind my back,

cheated without shame,

and eventually turned violent.

The first time he hit me, shock froze my body.
The second time, fear settled in.
The third time, I realized I was living in a nightmare I helped write.

One night, he locked me in our bedroom, held me hostage behind a door I couldn't open.
My cries didn't move him.
My fear didn't soften him.

But God heard me.

He sent my brother like a warrior through the night.
My brother kicked that door open, shattering wood, boundaries, and fear.
He demanded that my ex let me go.

And in that moment, I saw what real covering looked like.

I left.
And this time, I didn't return.

We divorced.

The end of that marriage was painful,
but the breaking was also my awakening.

I finally understood something that saved my life:

You can't heal in the arms of the person who wounded you.
You can't find freedom in the room where you've been locked in.
You can't build purpose with someone who keeps breaking your peace.

Water-falling seasons teach you more than regret.
They teach endurance.
They teach discernment.
They teach you to love yourself more than you love the lies.

I didn't get it right…

but I got out.

And that was the beginning of everything God had for me next.

Scripture Reflection:

"When you go through deep waters, I will be with you."

— Isaiah 43:2 (NLT)

CHAPTER 6

Missing Ingredients

There was a season when hope slipped through my fingers like sand,
when self-esteem was something I wore like a mask,
smiling on the outside while my heart whispered its exhaustion underneath.

I had left a broken marriage,
escaped the violence,
survived the lies,
and stepped into a new chapter…
but healing is not automatic.
Leaving doesn't mean the wounds close overnight.

I tried to start over.
Tried to rebuild.
Tried to convince myself that I was fine.

But something was missing.
Not just something—
many things.
Prayer.
Praise.
Presence.
Purpose.

Two of the most essential ingredients of my life, my prayer life and my praise had quietly slipped out of my hands while I was busy trying to hold everything else together.

I didn't notice it at first.
I still believed in God.
I still talked to Him.
I still felt Him…
but I wasn't seeking Him.
I wasn't feeding my spirit.
I wasn't protecting my heart.
I wasn't tending to the wounds that needed His touch.
I was focused on finding love in all the wrong places,
pouring from an empty cup,
trying to fill voids that only God could heal.
I didn't see the spiritual starvation happening inside me.
But God did.
He watched me chase after relationships that weren't meant to hold me.
He watched me run on fumes while pretending I had strength.
He watched me pour effort into everything except the very Source of my identity.
And He didn't shame me.
He didn't punish me.
He didn't turn away.
He simply waited, waited for me to remember where my true strength came from.
Missing ingredients will reveal themselves when life starts tasting bitter.
My life had become a mixture of exhaustion, disappointment, and quiet desperation.

I knew there was supposed to be more—

more joy,

more peace,

more meaning.

    But you cannot bake purpose with empty shelves.

You cannot rise spiritually without the yeast of prayer.

You cannot season your life with joy if praise is missing from your recipe.

    I had to return to the basics…

to the things that kept me grounded,

the things that restored me,

the things that reminded me who I was before heartbreak tried to rename me.

    I had to return to God.

    Not the God I visited only in crisis,

but the God who had carried me through every storm,

the God who saw me when I didn't see myself,

the God who held my life when I felt it slipping.

    And the moment I began to seek Him again,

the ingredients started coming back:

Hope.

Joy.

Identity.

Direction.

Peace.

Worth.

Clarity.

Strength.

All the things I thought I lost were simply buried beneath the noise of everything I tried to carry alone.

Sometimes the missing ingredient… is you.

The version of you that remembers God.

The version of you that fights for peace.

The version of you that refuses to shrink.

The version of you that knows her life has flavor and purpose.

God wasn't waiting to punish me,

He was waiting to pour into me.

And when I returned to Him,

He returned to me everything I didn't know I needed.

Scripture Reflection:

"Draw near to God, and He will draw near to you."

— James 4:8 (NKJV)

CHAPTER 7
Finding My Voice

Before I ever found the courage to speak, I learned how to sing.

Music became the language that held all the words I didn't yet know how to say. It was expression, escape, therapy, and prophecy wrapped into melody. Music didn't judge me, it carried me. When my voice trembled in life, it stood strong in song.

After everything I had endured—heartbreak, broken homes, broken promises, music became the first place where I could breathe again.

When I moved to St. Louis, Missouri, it became a season of transition, rebuilding, and rediscovery. My mother kept my baby boy until I could settle in, work, and stabilize my new life. I hustled hard; full-time work by day, singing part-time by night. It was the beginning of a woman reclaiming her identity.

And that's where I met my second husband.

He was preparing to return to active duty in the Army, and little did I know that meeting him would mark a chapter filled with love, loss, travel, growth, and spiritual awakening. We married and moved to Texas, where I gave birth to my second child, my baby girl, my mirror, my blessing whose first breath came with her first word:

"Mom."

Right there in the delivery room, she spoke to me.
And even now, I believe God allowed that word to be her first so I would never forget that I was chosen to mother her with strength and tenderness.

Our life took us across the world to places like Germany, Berlin, Italy.

Some women discover themselves in silence.
I found myself under lights, behind microphones, and in front of audiences who had no idea that each note I sang carried pieces of my past.

I sang with purpose.
I sang with emotion.
I sang to survive.
I sang until the brokenness began to lift.

But even in a new country and a new life, cracks formed in our marriage.
This time, it wasn't because I wasn't loving, nurturing, or committed. I held my home, my children, and my responsibilities close. But I had buried a truth deep inside:

When I first met him… I did not love him.

Love grew over time.
But eventually, so did the distance.
And just like before, the familiar sting of lies, cheating, and broken trust resurfaced.

Except this time…

I wasn't the same woman.
I wasn't overwhelmed.
I wasn't shattered.
I wasn't drowning.
I was stronger.
Wiser.

More aware.

More spiritually grounded.

And I could sing my way through the pain.

The marriage ended after ten years—but I didn't end with it.

I felt closer to God than I had in years. My voice, the very gift that carried me became my strength, my prayer, and my shield.

We eventually relocated to Florida, and that was where the marriage dissolved completely.

But the ending became my beginning.

I packed up my life and moved back to Texas,

not as a broken woman,

not as a victim,

but as a woman ready to build again.

And this time, I built something beautiful:

a salon.

Not just a business, but a sanctuary of love, prayer, sisterhood, and belonging.

Clients came for haircare, but they left with peace.

They shared their secrets, their burdens, their celebrations, their heartbreaks and little did they know, God was working through my hands and my voice.

I fasted for them.

I prayed with them.

I shouted praises with them.

I cried with them.

I spoke life over them.

I celebrated their victories.

The songs that filled the salon traveled across the city, and soon people were saying:

"There's a praying woman over there."

"She sings heaven down."

"She pours into you while she does your hair."

"You walk out feeling lighter."

"You walk out feeling loved."

Finding my voice wasn't just about singing.

It was about becoming.

A woman who could minister without a pulpit.

A woman who could speak life without a microphone.

A woman who could create healing spaces with her hands, her words, and her presence.

My voice wasn't found on a stage; it was found in surrender.

It was found in truth.

It was found in worship.

It was found in the women I served.

It was found in the God who kept calling me back to Him.

This chapter of my life wasn't just about music.

It was about becoming the woman God always intended me to be.

Scripture Reflection:

"He put a new song in my mouth, a hymn of praise to our God."

— Psalm 40:3 (NIV)

CHAPTER 8

Standing in the Gap

Texas was more than a place for me,

it was a season.

A season of rebuilding,

replanting,

and rediscovering who I was in God.

I was singing, working, traveling, ministering, and pouring into women while still learning how to pour into myself. My salon had become my sanctuary, a place where hair was restored, hearts were comforted, and prayer flowed as freely as conversation. But even with all the blessings God sprinkled across my life, there was one thing I knew for certain:

I did not want another man.

I had prayed hard the kind of prayer that rises from a woman who has been hurt too deeply, too often.

"Lord, keep me busy."

And oh, He did.

"Lord, take away the desire for any man."

And for a long while… He did that too.

I wasn't confused about who I was.

I wasn't wrestling with identity.

I was simply a woman who had survived too much to gamble with her heart again.

I told God, "I hate men."
Not out of bitterness,
but out of exhaustion from the damage they had caused.
I felt safe in my solitude.
Strong in my independence.
Whole in my healing.
"I'm good," I said.
And I meant it.
But healing has a way of softening you…
and God has a way of interrupting your declarations with His plans.
One day, a different kind of prayer slipped from my lips:
"Lord… if You ever decide to send me a man, keep my desires on hold until it's the right man the one You choose, the one praying for a woman like me."
I didn't know it then, but heaven had already responded.
And God sent him…
straight into my salon.
He walked in asking for pedicure and manicure services—
services I didn't even offer.
I pointed him next door, but instead of leaving, he lingered…
talking, smiling, trying to stretch the moment just a little longer.
I didn't feel sparks.
No butterflies.
No "oh, that's him" moment.
And let's be honest, his bald head and gold teeth did not register as "husband material."

But he saw something in me...
something God whispered into his spirit long before I recognized it myself.

Three days later, we crossed paths again.
Not at the salon.
Not in a store.
But at the **post office**—
at the exact same time.

When he saw me, he ran across the street like he was running toward a promise.
He asked me to have lunch with him.
Not a date.
Not romance.
Just lunch.

I still didn't see him as "fresh meat."
I was dormant, emotionally neutral, relationally uninterested.
But something in me, perhaps God Himself told me to say yes.
So, I did.

Three months later, on Christmas Day...
just like a present wrapped in heaven...
I became his lady.

Not his "girlfriend."
He never called me that.
He said, **"my lady."**
A title that held honor, care, and intention.

He did everything differently.

He opened doors.

He showed respect.

He led with consistency.

He made his interest known without confusion.

He pursued me the way a man does when God is guiding his steps.

    Then came the moment that still makes me laugh.

    Before we officially became a couple, I asked if I could come over to use his computer late one evening.

He said, "Sure, the door will be unlocked. Just let yourself in."

    So, I sat there responding to emails, focused on my work, when suddenly

out of the corner of my eye, I saw a shadow moving closer.

    My heart jumped!

Fear rose.

That fighter in me stood up and said, *"Try me if you want to."*

    I braced myself—ready to swing, ready to defend, ready to call heaven and 911 at the same time.

    But when I turned around, what I saw made me exhale in relief…

    He wasn't creeping toward me.

He wasn't trying anything.

He wasn't even paying attention to me.

    He was kneeling beside his bed—

head bowed,

hands clasped,

praying before going to sleep.

    And in that moment,

God whispered:

"This is the man who will stand in the gap for you.

The one I prepared.

The one who prays.

The one who covers.

The one who loves differently."

Nothing about him matched what I imagined...
but everything about him matched what I prayed.

The gap between heartbreak and healing—

he stood in it.

The gap between my past and my promise—

he stood in it.

The gap between the woman I was and the woman I was becoming—

he stood in it.

This wasn't just a love story.

It was a redemption story.

A God story.

A reminder that when God sends someone,

He sends them with purpose.

From that day forward, the Lord made sure I knew:

I was never standing alone.

Scripture Reflection:

"I sought the Lord, and He heard me; He delivered me from all my fears."

— Psalm 34:4 (NKJV)

CHAPTER 9

More Than a Woman

There comes a moment in every woman's journey when she looks at her life,
not just the painful chapters,
not just the hard roads,
but the whole of who she is and realizes:

I am more than what I've been through.
More than what I survived.
More than what tried to break me.
More than a woman…
I am God's masterpiece.

This season felt like stepping into sunlight after years of walking through shadows. I could feel God's presence in every part of my day—in my work, my home, my children, my voice, and in the way my spirit finally breathed without restriction.

People noticed it before I fully understood it myself.

Strangers would stop me in grocery store aisles, their faces soft with wonder:

"Ma'am… angels walk with you."

Others would say,

"I remember you from St. James — you sang heaven down."

Their words didn't inflate me; they awakened me.
It wasn't pride.
It wasn't ego.
It was recognition.

God was on me.
Not because I was flawless,
not because I had everything figured out,
but because I had walked through fire
and come out dressed in purpose.

My children, the ones who witnessed my battles, breakdowns, breakthroughs, and rebuilding became my greatest confirmations.

My son would say,

"Mom, you're the best mother. You always have been."
Words I didn't always feel worthy of,
but words my heart desperately needed.

And my daughter—
my artistic, expressive, sunshine-souled girl would fill my world with handwritten notes, colored drawings, and tender messages.

She would say,

"Mom, you're my hero."
And I kept every one of them,
because every stroke and every word felt like healing.

These weren't just compliments.

They were **affirmations**.
Divine reminders that I had grown into the woman God always envisioned.

I felt myself moving in rhythm with Heaven.

My thoughts weren't just mine—they were clearer, wiser, stronger, Spirit-led.

My decisions felt guided.

My steps felt ordered.

My heart felt anchored.

This was my sweet space—

my sacred alignment—

the place where I wasn't just connected to God…

I was walking with Him.

For the first time in my life,

I knew who I was.

Not just Patricia.

Not just Patrice.

Not just "mama."

Not just a singer, stylist, or servant-hearted woman.

I was more…

so much more.

A daughter.

A sister.

A granddaughter.

A cousin.

An aunt.

A friend.

A mother.

A grandmother.

A great-grandmother.

A mother-in-law.

A wife.

But beyond all of that…

I am a child of God.

I am loved by Him.

I am chosen by Him.

I am carried by Him.

I am more than a woman—

I am His woman.

This was the season where God leaned close and whispered:

"You are everything I created you to be.

Everything you thought you lost, I restored.

Everything others tried to break, I rebuilt.

Everything you surrendered, I blessed."

And for the first time, not just as a mother, a wife, a creator, or a friend,

but as Patricia,

I felt whole.

Scripture Reflection:

"She is clothed with strength and dignity, and she laughs without fear of the future."

— **Proverbs 31:25 (NIV)**

CHAPTER 10
Problem to Purpose

By the time I reached this chapter of my life, I was no longer the woman searching for love.
No longer the woman fighting for belonging.
No longer the woman trying to mend the pieces others had broken.

I was living my blessed life—
whole, grounded, healed, and finally walking in the light God had been pulling me toward all along.

But before I became a wife again, before God placed that final piece of partnership into my life, there was one more truth He needed to settle deep inside me:

The difference between a problem and a purpose.

My husband and I had been dating for a year when he decided it was time.
Time to shift from courting to covenant.
Time to move from companionship to commitment.
Time to seal what God had already ordained.

And let me tell you how it happened, because it still makes me smile.

He had everything planned.
A whole crew of people waited at his friend's house for the big proposal.
He had the moment mapped out, imagined, rehearsed.

But that's not how it went.

Somewhere between anticipation and excitement,
right at a gas station of all places,
he just couldn't hold it in.

He asked me to marry him then and there —
simple, sincere, unexpected.

And I said yes.

But then —
just for a moment —
fear tried to weave its way back in.

Not fear of him.
Not fear of marriage.
But fear of **me**.

Fear of my past.
Fear of patterns.
Fear of getting it wrong again.
Fear of repeating what nearly destroyed me.
Fear of failing God after finally being restored.

My mind tried to resurrect old wounds:
whispers of unworthiness,
whispers of doubt,
whispers of *"What if…?"*

But fear does not get the final say when God is the One writing the chapter.

That fear didn't last long.
Not after everything the Lord had brought me through.

Right in the middle of my worry, the narrow path of righteousness appeared in my spirit—the same path God had been guiding me toward through every trial, every tear, every transformation.

I could feel Him pulling me forward, steadying me, whispering:

"You are the one.
This is the promise.
Walk boldly."

And as God often does, He used the right man with the right words at the right time.

My husband—

Lord have mercy—

is a verbal charm gymnast.

He can flip a sentence, stretch a compliment, leap over doubt, and land flat-footed in reassurance without missing a beat.

One well-placed phrase from him can silence a whole storm.

And that day, he said exactly what I needed to hear…

exactly how I needed to hear it…

and those doubts folded like weak paper.

In his words, his desire, his consistency, and his intentionality, I felt God Himself reminding me:

"You are not a problem.
You have purpose."

My husband didn't just choose me—

God sent him to confirm me.

To remind me that love after pain is possible.

That covenant after chaos is possible.

That joy after sorrow is possible.

That purpose after problems is not only possible—

it's promised.

He came into my life at the exact moment God ordained.

Not a minute early.

Not a moment late.

Placed.

Positioned.

Predestined.

Purposeful.

When I said "*yes*,"

not just at the gas station,

not just in front of a crowd,

but yes in my **spirit**—

I stepped into a destiny that had been waiting on me.

A destiny where love wasn't a lesson…

but a blessing.

A destiny where partnership wasn't pain…

but peace.

A destiny where I was no longer someone trying to survive…

but a woman **standing firm in purpose.**

The man is mine.

Because God said:

"It is time."

Scripture Reflection:

"He makes all things work together for the good of those who love Him and are called according to His purpose."

— **Romans 8:28 (NLT)**

CHAPTER 11
Shaping Faith

Marriage is a beautiful thing—
but it is also a place where your faith gets tested, stretched, and reshaped in unexpected ways.

We were married on Christmas Day—
a date wrapped in holiness, joy, and divine new beginnings.

We didn't know then that our dear friend and pastor, Dr. Riley—now resting with the Lord—had also been married on Christmas Day more than fifty years before.

When he heard the news, he let out one of those deep, soul-warming laughs and said,

"Well then… y'all are already walking in favor. Christmas weddings last!"

He loved us.
He prayed for us.
He covered our marriage with wisdom, humor, and blessing.

One of his favorite lines was:

"Sons, if you want your marriage to last… remember: in the sight of God, the woman is always right."

My husband would grin every time.

But once the wedding glow faded,
once ceremony turned into daily life,
once silence replaced celebration…

I found myself wrestling with something unexpected:

How do I pray out loud in my own home without feeling exposed?
How do I invite my husband into my sacred space?
How do we begin praying together?

Prayer had always been my refuge—
my hiding place,
my healing place,
my anchor,
my weapon.

It was intimate.
It was personal.
It was mine.

So merging prayer with marriage felt vulnerable…
almost too vulnerable.

It wasn't that I feared my husband.
I feared what prayer reveals—
the raw truth,
the deep wounds,
the unfiltered honesty of my heart.

So, I started small.
Whispered prayers in the morning.
Silent petitions while cooking.
Little worship moments tucked into the corners of everyday life.

And slowly…
God began drawing us closer.

Then came the turning point, a moment when trust grew tall enough to bring prayer into the center of our union.

    We sat down one evening,

open, honest, and ready for deeper connection,

and we talked about praying together **every day**.

    Not occasionally.

Not only in crisis.

Not just before bed.

    But daily.

Consistently.

As a covenant.

    So, we made that covenant—

right then, right there—

promising to pray together no matter what came our way.

    And my husband…

Lord, You truly outdid Yourself with him.

    He became the spiritual leader of our home.

He began blessing meals,

praying over gatherings,

covering family moments,

and lifting every occasion before God—

unless he asked someone else to pray.

    And each morning, without fail,

he would wake up and *bee-line straight to the prayer room* in our home.

    No hesitation.

No wandering.

Straight to God.

    Watching him—

a man with a bald head and gold teeth whom I once thought was creeping up on me—

kneel before the Lord

became one of the most beautiful, humbling sights of my life.

It was confirmation.

Affirmation.

Alignment.

Our faith didn't just grow individually—

it grew together.

We prayed as one.

We worshipped as one.

We sought God as one.

We strengthened each other spiritually,

encouraged one another,

and built a home where God wasn't just welcomed—

He was the foundation.

What I once feared became the sweetest part of our marriage.

Prayer didn't make us perfect,

it made us connected.

It made us peaceful.

It made us anchored.

It made us whole.

Dr. Riley used to say,

"A marriage with God in the middle cannot fall."

And now I know…

he was absolutely right.

Our covenant of daily prayer didn't just shape our faith—

it reshaped our marriage.

Scripture Reflection:

"Unless the Lord builds the house, the builders labor in vain."
— Psalm 127:1 (NIV)

CHAPTER 12

Turning Struggle Into Strength

No matter how beautiful the beginning,
every marriage eventually faces a season that tests its roots.

I didn't expect ours to hit so soon.

After the joy, the covenant of prayer, the laughter, the alignment, and the peace—
there came a shift.
Not a big argument.
Not an explosion.
Not a betrayal.

Just a slow, quiet drift that crept in without warning.

The wooing faded.
The compliments grew scarce.
His tone grew sharper, quicker, more demanding.
The tenderness softened into routine.
And the weight of responsibility began quietly shifting onto my shoulders.

I felt it—
deeply, quietly, constantly.

Frustration grew.
Appreciation felt distant.
Excitement dissolved into monotony.

I wanted to speak…
but I didn't want to hurt him.

Didn't want to sound ungrateful.

Didn't know how to open a door I wasn't sure how to close.

But silence is a dangerous place for a married heart.

While I was feeling alone,
he was unaware—
still living, still moving, still talking with friends and family
more than he talked with me.

Days turned into weeks.
Weeks turned into months.

And in those months, insecurities whispered:

"What if someone else caught his attention?"
"What if someone could catch mine?"

I wasn't planning to cheat—
but I needed to understand the thoughts,
the loneliness,
the hunger for affection.

Before anything dangerous could take root,
I sat down with him.

And I told the truth:

"I feel bored.

I feel neglected.

And I feel like I want to cheat."

It wasn't a threat.
It was a cry for connection.

He didn't yell.

He didn't accuse.

He didn't storm away.

But he did get quiet.

And for **three long days**

we barely spoke.

Our words were dry.

Our greetings were cold.

No prayer.

No warmth.

Just two hurting hearts sitting in a fog neither of us wanted to be in.

But on the fourth day—

God intervened.

My husband asked me to sit down.

This time, it was his turn to speak.

He told me how my words shook him.

How blindsided he felt.

How he also felt neglected.

How he missed things I used to do and say.

How he too wondered why our tenderness had faded.

And in that moment,

God held up a mirror.

The truth wasn't that he stopped loving me.

Or that someone else caught his eye.

Or that something was broken beyond repair.

The truth was simple and humbling:

Life shifted…

and we forgot to shift with it.

I was focused on what I wasn't receiving.

He was focused on what he wasn't receiving.

We were both waiting to feel something

we had stopped giving.

Love is a cycle—

and what stops flowing out

eventually stops flowing in.

So, we made a decision—

a grown-up, covenant-level, heart-level decision:

Choose each other.

Again.

On purpose.

With intention.

With humility.

With honesty.

We got back on the saddle.

Back into prayer.

Back into communication.

Back into connection.

Back into "us."

God allowed the struggle—

not to break us,

but to strengthen us.

Because faith without testing is theory.

Love without challenge is fantasy.

A marriage without storms is fragile.

But a marriage that survives struggle?

That's a marriage shaped by God's hands.

We hit a rocky road.
We walked through cloudy days.
We navigated silence and confusion.

But then God—
as He always does—
turned our struggle into strength.

He turned our miscommunication
into deeper understanding.

He turned our drifting
into recommitment.

He turned our fears
into intimacy.

He turned our "what ifs"
into "we will."

And we did.
We do.
We choose.
We remain.

Every day,
we choose each other.

And that is the strength
that struggle built.

Scripture Reflection:

"My grace is sufficient for you, for My strength is made perfect in weakness."
— 2 Corinthians 12:9 (NKJV)

CHAPTER 13

Partnership & Peace

Every morning, I rise with one intention in my heart:
to stay in partnership with God.

Not halfway.

Not sometimes.

Not only when life is gentle.

But every single day.

My heart redirects itself back to prayer and purpose.

It's a rhythm now—

a sacred routine.

"Lord, create in me a clean heart.

Renew a right spirit within me.

Make me a new creature."

And He does—

over and over again.

Because when God becomes your true Partner,

you stop fighting battles in your own strength.

You stop reacting to every distraction.

You stop falling apart when storms rise without warning.

You stop letting fear dictate your decisions or your peace.

When you stay aligned with God,

nothing that comes your way—

not death,

not disappointment,

not trauma,

not loss,

not chaos,

not the enemy's whispers,

not the devil's traps—

can dismantle the peace He planted inside you.

    I learned something powerful:

Partnership with God is not quiet.

    It isn't passive.

It isn't just believing.

    It is **active.**

Intentional.

Daily.

Grounded.

Unmovable.

Steady.

    It means choosing God when I feel strong

and choosing Him just as fiercely when I feel tired.

    It means handing Him my distractions

before they root themselves in my spirit.

    It means trusting Him when something unforeseen

tries to steal, kill, or destroy the peace He established in me.

    This partnership with God—

this covenant with my Creator—

is what sustains my home,

my mind,

my marriage,

my children,

my identity,

my calling,

and my peace.

There was a time when peace felt temporary—
conditional, shaky, and easily shattered.

But not anymore.

Now I walk with a peace that surpasses all understanding.
A peace that doesn't make sense to outside observers.
A peace that doesn't crumble under pressure.
A peace that sits me down and whispers:

"Daughter, you are covered."

And part of that covering
is the man God entrusted to my life.

A man transformed by the renewing of his mind.
A man who loves God first,
so he can love himself well,
and love me wholly.
A man who values peace because he knows the Prince of Peace.

He wakes up and bee-lines to the prayer room—
not out of duty,
but out of desire.

He understands that any marriage thriving in Christ
is a marriage that will outlive storms.

What more could I ask for?

We often look at each other,
with quiet smiles and sincere hearts, and say:

"We have the greatest Partner ever known to mankind."

Not because we are perfect.

Not because we never face struggle.

Not because we never disagree.

But because God Himself sits at the center of our home—

in the center of our hearts,

our decisions,

our growth,

our healing,

our covenant.

Partnership with God birthed peace.

Peace birthed strength.

Strength birthed unity.

Unity birthed joy.

This chapter of my life is not built on survival.

It is built on surrender.

It is built on agreement.

It is built on alignment.

We are partners in life,

and we are at peace—

because our greatest Partner is Jesus.

When God is your foundation,

you don't fall—

you flourish.

Scripture Reflection:

"**You will keep him in perfect peace, whose mind is stayed on You, because he trusts in You.**"

— Isaiah 26:3 (NKJV)

CHAPTER 14

Peeling the Promises

There are seasons in life when God doesn't just stretch you —
He strips you.
Not to harm you,
but to heal you.
Not to punish you,
but to purify you.
Not to overwhelm you,
but to reroute you back to purpose.
I call this season the peeling.
This was the part of my journey where life circled back around —
not to repeat the pain,
but to recycle the transformation.
On the outside, I looked blessed, stable, happy, complete. I was traveling with my husband, thriving in marriage, singing, serving, loving, learning, and walking in the fullness of God's purpose.
But inside? My body was waving red flags like a referee at a championship game.
My health started acting up with no warning. My heart rate dropped low. My stress level shot up high. My energy disappeared like a vanishing act. My body felt foreign. And fear crept in fast.
I didn't know what was happening. All I knew was: "This feels like a life-or-death situation."
My primary care physician did not take it lightly. She sent me to every specialist she could think of:

- Neuropathy specialist
- Orthopedic doctor
- Ultrasound technician
- Nerve specialist

Test after test.

Referral after referral.

Appointment after appointment.

And while all of this was happening…

my poor husband — Lord bless him — was being patient in places most men would have panicked.

Because let me be honest:

the V-Jay-Jay was NOT singing any kind of song.

No soprano, no alto, no harmony, no ad-libs.

SILENCE.

The choir was closed.

He was supportive, kind, and understanding…

but we both knew something wasn't right.

Then — here comes God.

Not through a diagnosis.

Not through a lab result.

Not through a specialist.

But through a whisper to my spirit:

"Daughter, this is not a medical emergency. It is a spiritual peeling."

And layer by layer, He began to show me why my body was shutting down:

Layer 1: Stress.

I was carrying more in my mind than my body could sustain.

Layer 2: Procrastination.

Putting off meaningful things was creating internal chaos.

Layer 3: Poor eating habits.

What I put in my body did not match the assignment on my life.

Layer 4: Late nights.

Rest was not a priority; it was an afterthought.

Layer 5: Graduate school overload.

I was pouring out academically but not filling myself spiritually or physically.

Layer 6: Laziness that creeped in quietly.

Not because I didn't care, but because I didn't slow down enough to function with purpose.

And the Lord said:

"You cannot pour from an empty vessel,

and you cannot thrive in purpose with unhealthy patterns."

My body wasn't failing me.

It was warning me.

It was tapping out.

It was pleading with me to slow down, sit down, breathe, listen, and reset.

And God made it clear:

"I need YOU back.

Your husband needs you.

Your purpose needs you.

You need you."

So, I surrendered —

not to fear,

but to alignment.

I asked God to show me the way back to health, wholeness, and holy discipline. And like He always does, He guided me:

- Better eating
- Better rest
- Better time management
- Better boundaries
- Better balance
- Better stewardship of my physical temple

And as my mind, body, and spirit realigned…

Something beautiful happened.

Morning glory returned.

Yes, Lord — restored!

The choir came back.

The notes were back on key.

The marriage melody was revived.

And my husband was patiently grateful.

This season taught me something priceless:

Healing is not always medical.

Sometimes it is spiritual.

Sometimes it is behavioral.

Sometimes it is emotional.

Sometimes it is God saying,

"Daughter, I need to peel you…

To restore you."

And He did.

Faith grew stronger.

Purpose became clearer.

My marriage blossomed again.

My body regained strength.

My peace returned.

And my joy found its rhythm.

When God peels layers,
He reveals promises.

And every promise He peeled back
was wrapped in His love.

Scripture Reflection:

"Beloved, I pray that you may prosper in all things and be in good health, just as your soul prospers." — 3 John 1:2 (NKJV)

CHAPTER 15

Seeing the Blessings of God

There comes a point in life when blessings no longer look like big moments, loud miracles, or mountaintop breakthroughs. Instead, they look like breath. Movement. Awareness. Peace. Presence. Simplicity. Clarity. And gratitude.

I've reached that point.

These days, when I wake up in the morning, I can hardly wait to thank God.

Not because everything is perfect.

Not because life is without challenges.

But because I woke up.

That alone is a blessing.

Before I even stand, before I touch a toothbrush or sip a glass of water, I pause.

Because the moment my eyes open — He has already shown Himself faithful.

Then my feet hit the floor.

And that's another blessing.

I wiggle my toes — blessing.

I stretch my arms — blessing.

I sit up without help — blessing.

I breathe without effort — blessing.

I walk to the restroom — blessing.

I can still sing, think, love, and laugh — blessing.

When you've lived the life I've lived,

when you've survived what I've survived,

when you've cried the tears I've cried,

fought the battles I've fought, and overcome the obstacles that tried to take you out…

You learn to recognize blessings that other people overlook.

I realized something powerful:

The blessings of God start with me—

my attitude, my gratitude, my perspective, my willingness to see Him in everything.

And those blessings?

They don't just stop with me.

They flow through me.

To my husband.

To my children.

To my grandchildren.

To my great-grandchildren.

To the women I minister to.

To the people I interact with.

To every person God positions in my path.

I count it all joy to be in the presence of blessed people —

not because of their cars, houses, degrees, or titles,

but because of their light,

their spirit,

their peace,

their faith,

their story,

their testimony.

Blessings recognize blessings.

Blessed people glow from the inside out, and I thank God that I can see it because I finally see it in myself.

God's blessings are not random.

They are deliberate.

Intentional.

Strategic.

Personal.

Tailored.

Timely.

Overflowing.

He doesn't just bless me for me.

He blesses me so I can be a blessing to someone else.

So, I can speak life.

Serve with joy.

Give with purpose.

Love with grace.

Encourage with sincerity.

And walk in alignment with Him.

Every breath is a reminder that God's hand is still on my life.

Every sunrise whispers, "I'm not finished with you."

Every step I take declares victory.

Every piece of peace I carry announces that God lives in me.

And the longer I live,

the more I realize that blessings aren't big —

they're constant.

Unfolding.

Multiplying.

Flowing.

Revealing.

Shaping.

Sustaining.

I see God's blessings everywhere.

Because now, I see Him in everything.

Scripture Reflection:

"Every good and perfect gift is from above." — James 1:17 (NIV)**

CHAPTER 16
Built for B-E-A-U-T-Y

Life has taught me many things,

but the greatest of them is this:

We were created in beauty —

the beauty of God's own image.

Not beauty defined by mirrors, makeup, or milestones,

but beauty defined by purpose, process, and presence.

Beauty that breathes.

Beauty that breaks and rises again.

Beauty that grows, shifts, heals, and awakens.

Beauty that reflects the Truth, the Way, and the Light.

When I look back over my life —

the childhood trauma,

the secrets,

the heartbreaks,

the marriages,

the moves,

the miracles,

the births,

the losses,

the healing,

the revelation —

I see BEAUTY everywhere.

Not because the path was easy.

Not because the journey was flawless.

But because God was in every step.

And no matter what tried to destroy me,

God whispered:

"Daughter, you were built for this."

He formed me in purpose.

He sustained me in struggle.

He lifted me in weakness.

He restored me in brokenness.

He planted me in faith.

He crowned me in truth.

And He allowed me to become

the woman I was always destined to be.

Not perfect.

Not polished.

But BEAUTIFUL — in the most divine way.

So, in this final chapter,

I offer you the word that defines my life

and will now define yours:

❀ B — Becoming

We are always becoming.

Becoming wiser.

Becoming stronger.

Becoming softer.

Becoming clearer.

Becoming the version of ourselves that God saw long before we did.

Becoming is a process —

not a destination.

E — Endurance

Every storm that should've broken you…

 you survived.

Every disappointment that tried to silence you…

you outgrew.

Every season that tried to bury you…

you rose from.

Endurance is the quiet proof

that God carried you even when you didn't feel Him.

A — Awakening

Awakening is the moment you realize

your life is not an accident —

it is an assignment.

It's when the spiritual veil lifts

and you begin to see life, love, purpose, and people

through God's eyes.

Awakening changes how you breathe,

how you walk,

how you pray,

how you speak,

how you love.

U — Unshakable

Not because you're strong on your own,

but because God strengthened you.

Unshakable peace.

Unshakable faith.

Unshakable mind.

Unshakable identity.

Life may rock your boat,

but it cannot sink a woman anchored in God.

T — Transformation

Transformation is not about improving —

it's about becoming completely new.

The Bible says,

"Be transformed by the renewing of your mind,"

and that is exactly what God did in you:

He renewed your mind.

He restored your joy.

He refined your purpose.

He rebuilt your heart.

Transformation is the evidence

that God still makes miracles out of messes.

Y — Yahweh's Reflection

This is the highest truth of all:

You are the reflection of God.

Not a mistake.

Not a broken vessel.

Not what you've been called,

Not what you survived,

Not what you feared.

You are Yahweh's creation.

Yahweh's daughter.

Yahweh's masterpiece.

Yahweh's light.

Yahweh's reflection.

Everything about you —

your strength, your voice, your faith, your love, your healing —

reflects Him.

And that, my dear reader,

is BEAUTY.

Life as we once knew it is beautiful.

Life as we live it now is divine.

And the life God destined for us?

It is eternal.

So, walk boldly.

Walk freely.

Walk joyfully.

Walk purposefully.

Because you —

and every woman who reads these pages —

were not just built for beauty.

You were built from Beauty Himself.

In His image.

For His glory.

With His hands.

By His love.

And that is the final truth of this story.

Scripture Reflection:

"I praise You because I am fearfully and wonderfully made."
— Psalm 139:14 (NIV)

Scripture Index

Psalm 145:18 (NIV)
"The Lord is near to all who call on Him."
— Chapter 1

Daniel 2:22 (NKJV)
"He reveals deep and secret things; He knows what is in the darkness, and the light dwells with Him."
— Chapter 2

Psalm 27:10 (ESV)
"Though my father and mother forsake me, the Lord will take me in."
— Chapter 3

Proverbs 31:28 (NIV)
"Her children arise and call her blessed."
— Chapter 4

Isaiah 43:2 (NLT)
"When you go through deep waters, I will be with you."
— Chapter 5

James 4:8 (NKJV)
"Draw near to God, and He will draw near to you."
— Chapter 6

Psalm 40:3 (NIV)
"He put a new song in my mouth, a hymn of praise to our God."
— Chapter 7

Psalm 34:4 (NKJV)
"I sought the Lord, and He heard me; He delivered me from all my fears."
— Chapter 8

Proverbs 31:25 (NIV)
"She is clothed with strength and dignity, and she laughs without fear of the future."
— Chapter 9

Romans 8:28 (NLT)
"He makes all things work together for the good of those who love Him and are called according to His purpose."
— Chapter 10

Psalm 127:1 (NIV)
"Unless the Lord builds the house, the builders labor in vain."
— Chapter 11

2 Corinthians 12:9 (NKJV)
"My grace is sufficient for you, for My strength is made perfect in weakness."
— Chapter 12

Isaiah 26:3 (NKJV)
"You will keep him in perfect peace, whose mind is stayed on You, because he trusts in You."
— Chapter 13

3 John 1:2 (NKJV)
"Beloved, I pray that you may prosper in all things and be in good health, just as your soul prospers."
— Chapter 14

James 1:17 (NIV)
"Every good and perfect gift is from above."
— Chapter 15

Psalm 139:14 (NIV)
"I praise You because I am fearfully and wonderfully made."
— Chapter 16)

About the Author

Patricia A. Haynes is a woman shaped by resilience, faith, and the transformative power of truth. Born and raised in Mississippi, she learned early that silence carries its own language — a language she would one day translate into purpose. Through seasons of heartbreak, healing, and spiritual awakening, Patricia discovered her calling: to speak life, restore hope, and remind others that their stories are worthy of being told.

A mother, grandmother, wife, singer, counselor-in-training, and lifelong servant-leader, Patricia lives by the belief that God uses every chapter — even the broken ones — to reveal beauty. Her life reflects the message of this book: that purpose has a sound, healing has a voice, and every woman carries a language within her waiting to be spoken.

Today, Patricia continues to inspire others through her testimony, her service, and her unwavering devotion to God. *Language for Your Purpose* is her offering to every reader searching for meaning, courage, and the freedom to become who they were created to be.

Author Photographed by Eyes of the Beholder Photography.

www.ingramcontent.com/pod-product-compliance
Lightning Source LLC
Chambersburg PA
CBHW071240090426
42736CB00014B/3153